PERFORMANCE
EDITIONS

J.S. BACH
NINETEEN LITTLE PRELUDES

Edited and Recorded by Christos Tsitsaros

T0079186

To access companion recorded performances online, visit:
www.halleonard.com/mylibrary

Enter Code
8087-1232-3239-1785

On the cover:
*View of the New Market Place in
Dresden from the Moritzstrasse, 1749–1751*
by Bernardo Bellotto (1720–1780)
© Staatliche Kunstsammlungen Dresden
The Bridgeman Art Library International

ISBN 978-1-4234-8307-6

G. SCHIRMER, Inc.

DISTRIBUTED BY

7777 W. BLUEMOUND RD. P.O. BOX 13819 MILWAUKEE, WI 53213

www.musicsalesclassical.com
www.halleonard.com

CONTENTS

The price of this publication includes access to companion recorded performances online, for download or streaming, using the unique code found on the title page. Visit **www.halleonard.com/mylibrary** and enter the access code.

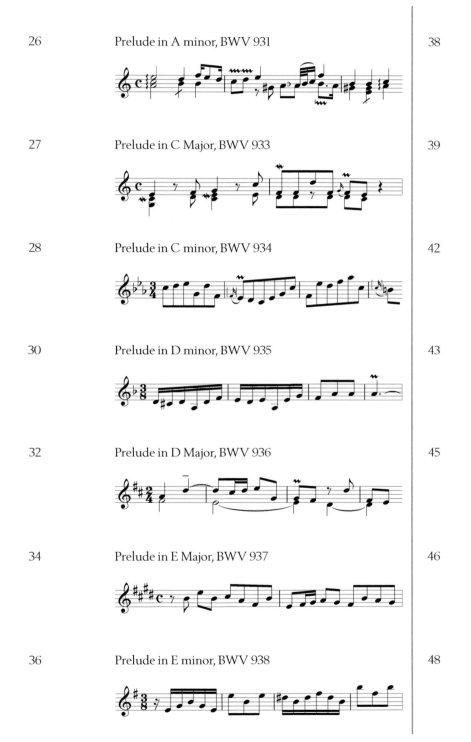

PERFORMANCE NOTES

A great master of the organ and the harpsichord, improviser, cantor and Kapellmeister, in addition to devoted family man, Johann Sebastian Bach also expanded his professional responsibilities in the area of education. Throughout his long musical career, he gave keyboard and composition lessons to his own children and other students. A strong emphasis in well-rounded musicianship was the staple of his keyboard instruction: in addition to exercises in finger agility, the session would include basics of *continuo* playing (realizing a figured bass line, then improvising freely on it), harmonization of chorales that led to formal composition, and finally study of repertoire. He would hierarchically assign the Inventions, followed by various movements from his Suites, and later some of the Preludes and Fugues from the *Well-Tempered Clavier.* He also exemplified different musical and technical problems with concise pieces created on the spot. When the student showed signs of boredom, Bach would spontaneously turn short musical ideas into "beautiful and expressive works of art." The preludes in this volume certainly belong in this category of work. The improvisational character of the genre with its perpetual motivic structure rooted in a chordal foundation provided Bach with an ideal vehicle for such spontaneous explorations.

The first seven preludes presented in this volume are drawn from the *Little Clavier Book* that Bach assembled around 1720 for the instruction of his eldest son, Wilhelm Friedemann, who at the time was a little over nine years old. Between 1717 and 1723, Bach served as Kapellmeister to Prince Leopold in Cöthen. Soon after he launched the *Clavier-Büchlein vor Wilhelm Friedemann Bach,* Wilhelm's mother died; it was not long before Bach married Anna Magdalena toward the end of 1721. Upon examining a facsimile of the manuscript, a mix of entries in both the handwritings of Johann Sebastian and his son supports the idea that the notebook had a double pedagogical function: that of an instrumental manual and a tool for composition studies pursued by Wilhelm under the guidance of his

father. We are to presume that most of the pieces in Wilhelm's handwriting were copied from his father's own originals. Some were inspired perhaps by Wilhelm himself but nevertheless supervised by his father, as the sporadic insertions in Bach's own hand indicate. In addition to the short preludes, the *Little Clavier Book* also encompassed a few dance movements, two chorales, eleven of the preludes of Book I of the *Well-Tempered Clavier* (some of which appear only in partial or less developed form), a series of fifteen pieces each entitled *Praeambulum,* and the Three-part Sinfonias, which in the notebook are designated as Fantasias. The last two, *Praeambula* and *Sinfonias,* form an early version of the 1723 Two-part Inventions and Three-part Sinfonias which Bach assembled just prior to moving from Cöthen to Leipzig.

The following set, *Six Little Preludes for Beginners,* arranged in a major-minor key order, exists only in copies made by Bach's pupils apparently after his death. BWV 939–943 appear in a manuscript copy of the *Little Clavier Book* made by the cantor Johann Peter Kellner. An additional gem, the Prelude in C minor, BWV 999, was intended for the lute as the indication *"pour la Lute"* suggests; however, it is equally suitable for keyboard and therefore is included in this edition.

Style and Interpretation

Ornamentation

The following table entitled "Explanation of Different Signs showing the correct manner of playing certain Ornaments" is featured in the opening pages of the *Clavier-Büchlein vor Wilhelm Friedemann Bach* in between a one-page nomenclature of notes and clefs and the *Applicatio,* a brief piece that exemplifies various ornaments and fingerings. The standard ornaments used by Bach in most of his keyboard music appear in this table, along with their corresponding name and full rhythmical realization.

TABLE OF ORNAMENTS

Explanation of Different Signs showing the correct manner of playing certain Ornaments
from the "Clavier-Büchlein vor Wilhelm Friedemann Bach"

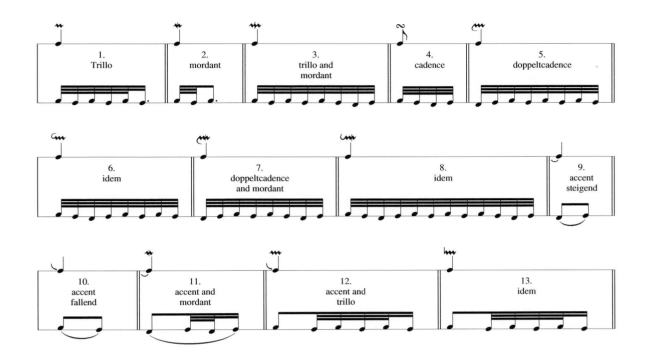

All ornaments in Bach's music, in accordance with performance practices of his time, are to be played on the beat. An exception to this rule is the half or short trill *(halb- or prall-triller)*, an ornament that occurs in stepwise descending motion. The note preceding the trill in this case is tied to the upper auxiliary note of the trill. Carl Philipp Emanuel Bach, in his *Essay on the True Art of Playing Keyboard Instruments*, states this ornament "...represents in miniature an enclosed, unsuffixed trill, introduced by either an appoggiatura or a principal note." Although not listed in the table of ornaments, it is nevertheless present in various preludes, such as the following excerpt.

Ex. 1: Prelude in E minor, BWV 938, mm. 13–15

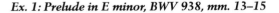

An interesting feature of Bach's ornamentation is the use of the trill with a mordent, or in C.P.E. Bach's terminology, "long trill with a suffix." As a rule, Bach uses this compound sign to indicate this particular ornament (example 2a), but occasionally he spells it with a trill sign followed by a fully written out termination (example 2b).

Ex. 2a: Prelude in C Major, BWV 924, mm. 3–4

Ex. 2b: Prelude in G minor, BWV 930, mm. 30–32

The trill (both short and long, with or without termination) and the mordent are the most frequent ornaments in the Little Preludes. An interesting version of the trill can be seen in the second of the *Six Little Prelude for Beginners* where the upper auxiliary note is notated as an appoggiatura followed by a trill. In this case, the succeeding trill would undoubtedly be of the half-trill type. The resulting four-note trill calls for a slight emphasis on the upper auxiliary, which melodically functions as a suspension.

Ex. 3: Prelude in C minor, BWV 934, mm. 1–2

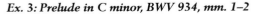

Similarly, appoggiaturas are notated in the traditional Italian form, with a grace note rather than the French-style parenthetical sign.

Ex. 4a: Prelude in C Major, BWV 933, m. 12

The seventh prelude from the *Little Clavier Book* is the only one in the series in which the appoggiaturas are notated in the French version appearing on the table.

Ex.4b: Prelude in A minor, BWV 931, mm. 5–7

Depending on the ability of the student, long trills can be performed unmeasured, as long as the left hand remains rhythmically stable. In the present edition, all long trills are realized in a metrically measured manner; however, as soon as the basic level of hand independence and finger ability is achieved, students may experiment with freer, faster-repetition trills, as in the following example.

Ex. 5: Prelude in D minor, BWV 935, mm. 3–5

The cadence (or "turn" in C.P. E. Bach's terminology) is an interesting ornament, lending itself as an alternative to the trill. Occurring between a note or appoggiatura and the following note, it can be realized in a variety of rhythmical ways, as seen in the following two examples.

Ex. 6a: Prelude in C Major, BWV 933, m. 4

Ex. 6b: Prelude in E Major, BWV 937, m. 19

The diagonal lines under certain chords, such as found in Prelude BWV 931, indicate that the chord should be broken with passing notes in between chord tones.

Ex. 7a: Prelude in A minor, BWV 931, m. 1

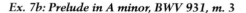

Ex. 7b: Prelude in A minor, BWV 931, m. 3

Tempo

In the pre-classical era, tempo was determined by cross-referencing the time signature, the prevailing texture, and internal rhythmic division of the movement. A piece that abounded in shorter rhythmic values (such as sixteenth and thirty-second notes), harmonic shifts, or more ornamentation was to be played comparatively slower than a metrically similar piece that featured longer note values (such as quarter or eighth notes), as well as fewer ornaments and harmonic shifts. According to C.P.E. Bach, the passages with the fastest notes are key points in determining the tempo, as they should be performed unhurriedly and distinctly. In various instances, he cautions the keyboardist against mechanical and hurried playing in fast movements, or "dragged" and "lethargic" in slow ones. Above all, he encourages players to think in terms of song in order to reach an understanding of the music. With these points in mind, the student should be encouraged to experiment with a range of speeds until an ideal tempo is reached, one that concurs with the musical content and technical demands, as well as the emotional aspect of the piece.

Considered in the context of character and affect, tempo becomes an integral expressive ingredient upon which all other factors such as articulation and dynamics depend. The following prelude offers a good example of how varying the tempo can evoke different emotions.

Ex. 8: Prelude in E minor, BWV 941, mm. 1–7

Tempo 1: Andante, ♩ = 104 (Mood: meditative, peaceful)
Tempo 2: Allegretto, ♩ = 121 (Mood: dance-like, uplifting)

The Prelude and *tempo rubato.*

An instrumental form akin to the toccata, the prelude was conceived in the sixteenth century as a short organ improvisation to indicate to the priest and the choir the starting pitch or the mode in which the music was to be sung. Later, it was adopted on the harpsichord to announce the key in which the ensuing piece would be played, as well as to try the instrument, test its tuning, and prepare the hands and fingers for the task. Louis Couperin's unmeasured Preludes perfectly illustrate the improvisational character of the genre, which is comprised of an underlying harmonic progression upon which a flourish motive is repeated, elaborated and "spun out" with each subsequent harmonic shift. As part of the foreword to his own measured Preludes in his treatise *L'Art de Toucher le Clavecin,* Louis' illustrious son, François, states: "A Prelude is a composition in which the fancy can free itself from all that is written in the book [...] It is necessary for those who will resort to the regulated preludes to play them freely without attaching too much precision to the movement; at least where I have not written the word *mesuré* ('measured')."

François Couperin's statement alludes to the use of *rubato* as befitting the extemporaneous character of the prelude. A useful time nuance consisting of a slight acceleration counterbalanced by a proportionate deceleration, *rubato* ("stolen time") may be deliberately adopted in the Little Preludes as well. Used sparingly at appropriate places, it will add interest to the performance by generating motion, highlighting key harmonic and melodic events, and conveying the whimsical character of the piece. Long virtuoso flourishes and pedal points lend themselves well for the use of rubato. Slight and well-balanced tempo deviations will provide direction and drive to the sequential passages typically found in such places.

Example 9: Prelude in C Major, BWV 924, mm. 9–18

In applying *rubato,* C.P.E. Bach warns the player to "keep the tempo at the end of the piece exactly the same as in the beginning." Therefore practicing the piece in an even, steady tempo is prerequisite before incorporating any kind of temporal freedom requiring taste, experience, and discipline.

Articulation

A sensible balance between the three important types of articulations mentioned in C.P.E. Bach's treatise is desirable for all of Bach's music, including the pieces of this volume. Those include the *legato, staccato,* and *portato* (also known as *non-legato.*) C.P.E. Bach and other theorists of the time inform us that the choice of articulation depended on the tempo and character of the music, the intervallic relations, and sometimes the melodic or harmonic function of the notes: "In general the briskness of allegros is expressed by detached notes and the tenderness of adagios by broad, slurred notes."

It is essential to interpret C.P.E. Bach's idea in the right context and to discern which notes to slur or detach, as well as the degree of detachment or connection. Howard Ferguson in his *Keyboard Interpretation from the 14th to the 19th Century* states: "The degree of staccato required is not always the same. It depends entirely on the context, and it may be anything from the shortest staccatissimo to a portato that is only one stage removed from staccato."

In general, the following easy rules may be followed in the Little Preludes:

1. Play the fastest note values *legato,* using a more articulated, crisper touch for faster tempos and a broader, lingering *legato* for slower tempos. This is in line with Bach's advice: "slurred notes appear in stepwise passages and in the slower or more moderate tempos."

2. In moderate or slower tempos, adopt *portato* articulation (a cross between *legato* and *staccato*) for longer values (such as quarter or eighth notes depending on the rhythmic structure.) In faster tempos, experiment with more *staccato* or a combination of *legato-staccato* for the longer note values.

3. Play all appoggiaturas (essentially stressed non-harmonic tones struck simultaneously with the bass) *legato* independently of tempo.

4. Use *non-legato* or *staccato* in larger intervals such as leaps of an octave. (This depends also on the tempo and prevailing mood.)

5. In slower and moderate tempos, one may prolong certain notes in broken chord figures over a part or the entire duration of the figure. C.P. E. Bach refers to this a special type of articulation as "tenuto."

Examples 10a and 10b demonstrate the aforementioned parameters.

Example 10a: Prelude in E minor, BWV 938, mm. 1–21

Example 10b: Prelude in C Major, BWV 933, mm. 1–5

Dynamics and Phrasing

C.P.E. Bach's ideal "rounded, pure, flowing manner of playing which makes for clarity and expressiveness" is achieved "when one hears all notes and embellishments played in correct time with fitting volume produced by a touch which is related to the true content of a piece." At the heart of this statement is the understanding of the true content of the composition, which forms the basis for all other parameters and expressive means. Later, C.P.E. Bach points out that "in order to arrive at an understanding of the true content and affect of a piece [...] it is advisable that every opportunity is seized to listen to soloists and ensembles."

As in the easier dance movements from the *Notebook for Anna Magdalena Bach* and other suite movements, various elements in the music can inform us on how to phrase and use dynamics effectively in order to bring the music to life, and showcase its melodic and harmonic contours. Some of these elements include:

1. The shape of the melody. A gradual increase or decrease of the volume helps enliven ascending and descending melodic gestures.

2. The use of tension-resolution effect. All dissonances such as appoggiaturas and suspensions need to be lightly stressed and resolved with a *diminuendo.*

3. The harmonic structure and form. A harmonic analysis will guide the player to place the right emphasis on denser chords and effectively indicate the direction of the harmonic progression or sequence. Certain preludes are divided into two sections, a formal element that calls for matching the dynamics shadings to the harmonic framework of the sections.

Texture is an additional consideration for the choice of dynamics and phrasing; in the Little Preludes it is more transparently delineated than in the early dances. A high degree of linearity, all horizontal levels participating thematically, sometimes conversing in imitation, or simply complementing each other requires an integral enunciation of the individual lines in their proper phrasing and articulation. The left hand lines often deserve more attention, their role being significantly more vital than a mere accompaniment.

In following these guidelines, the student should avoid a rigid approach to articulation. Variation within reasonable limits will help define the rhythmic aspect and highlight important melodic and harmonic events within the piece. The key to applying articulation is to make sure that it conforms to the character and tempo of the piece or passage, and that it stays within reach of the student's technical ability.

Fingering

C.P.E. Bach recounts that his father lived in an era when "a gradual but striking change in musical taste" was taking place. The strict polyphonic writing, possible with leaving the fingers on one position, was being infused and progressively replaced by more melodious writing, often spanning beyond the range of the five fingers. Such trends required experimentation with more than one way of fingering, especially ways that allowed for such passages to be played *legato* without stiffening the hand. It is precisely the need to accommodate new musical demands that prompted Bach "to devise a far more comprehensive fingering and especially to enlarge the role of the thumbs...." The thumb in Bach's time assumes a completely new role and forms "the key to all fingering." Its natural formation allows it to pass under the other fingers and act as a pivot enabling the other fingers to cross over. Crossing of longer fingers over short ones in scale passages was still quite common in Bach's time and was in fact amply used by him as well, as the short *Applicatio* in the *Little Clavier Book* suggests. This old fingering practice however was gradually substituted by the modern scale fingering, which allowed the thumb to pass under the second, third, and fourth fingers, and the same fingers to cross over the thumb. In the "new" system, the fifth finger is reserved for either the beginning of a stepwise passage or at the end of a run; both the thumb and the fifth finger are used mainly on white keys, except in wide stretches (such as in chord passages). For broken chord figures, C.P.E. Bach favors a fingering that conforms to the unbroken form of the chord. An example of this

can be in Prelude, BWV 930, one of three pieces where Bach's fingering is explicitly notated in the manuscript. The same rule can be adapted in most preludes through a systematic approach that entails the following steps:

1. Play broken chord figurations in their blocked form.
2. Think of how the various chords could be linked through fingering.
3. Apply the same fingering to the broken chord figures with due emphasis on connection between the various chords.

Following is an example of this line of work:

Example 11: Prelude in C minor, BWV 999, mm. 1–14

New-style fingering ideas, inspired by the more fashionable melodic writing of the times, are also present in Couperin's *L'Art de Toucher le Clavecin*. In his application of fingering, Couperin is concerned with preserving the legato. Following are three of Couperin's fingering ideas that are particularly useful in the Little Preludes:

1. Appoggiaturas preceded by the same note should be played with a different finger than the one used on the preceding note. The same rule applies when appoggiaturas are followed by four-note trills; this, since in stepwise motion the upper auxiliary of the trill, is a reiteration of the appoggiatura.
2. Series of trills are to be connected by means of fingering, silently changing the finger at the end of a trill. This rule may be adopted in passages other than ones containing series of trills.
3. Parallel thirds should be connected through fingering.

Notes on the Individual Preludes

Prelude in C Major, BWV 924

The dissonance-resolution effect resulting from suspensions embedded in the arpeggiated figures on the third or first beat of each measure provides the key to phrasing of this piece. At the same time, it is essential to maintain the long line and feeling of direction in the harmonic progression. The use of *rubato* will be helpful in mm. 9 to the end as a means to add motion and drive to the long cadenza-style flourish, which develops over the dominant pedal point.

Prelude in D minor, BWV 926

The phrasing of this piece can be thought from two different angles: either from the downbeat to the end of the next measure, or from the second eighth note to the downbeat. A synthesis of both these approaches will enhance the rhythmic drive and bring unity to the piece.

Prelude in F Major, BWV 927

A syncopated phrasing should start right from the beginning of the left-hand four-eighth-note group, lightly underlining the second eighth, which forms the beginning of the short motive. The lovely ascending bass lines in mm. 5–6 need to maintain their individuality amidst the arpeggiated chordal background in the right-hand part. Dynamic fluctuations here can be gauged by the suspension-resolution effect implied in the chord sequence. The accents on the ascending dominant seventh arpeggiated-figure in m. 14 leading to the culminating chord indicate a broadening of the tempo. Similarly, the frequent chord changes and syncopations in the last measure allude to an *allargando*, which will bring the piece to a dignified closure.

Prelude in G minor, BWV 930

In this rare example where Bach's own fingerings are included throughout, we note that the fingering of the arpeggiated figures conforms not only to their blocked form, but also to the way the chords relate to each other. An effort to create a physical connection with finger *legato* is evident throughout. A good example of the thumb being used as a pivot over which the other hand passes is in mm. 36–38.

Prelude in F Major, BWV 928

A combination of *portato* and *legato* will underline the suspensions in the counter theme. The simple harmonic frame of the motive (I-ii7-V-I) serves as a guide for phrasing. To ensure clarity and plasticity in the two-voice texture, it would be advisable to hold down the tied suspensions in the left hand all the way into the next note and to allow enough dynamic space between the two voices.

Prelude in D Major, BWV 925

As in the previous prelude, BWV 928, the underlying harmonic cadence (I-V-ii7-V7-I) indicates phrasing toward the denser chord (ii7) and rounding the resolution with a slight tempering of the sound. The syncopations of the counter theme are to be emphasized lightly in order to provide an interesting counter rhythm against the metric regularity of the sixteenth-note figures. Special care should be given to the dotted eighth notes followed by a sixteenth. The sixteenth should be fully articulated in its proper time and enunciated as part of the long singing line.

Prelude in A minor, BWV 931

The notation of the appoggiaturas in the French manner *(port de voix)* in mm. 6 and 8 of this prelude, and the frequent use of the *style brisé* (arpeggiated) in double notes and chords, point out to a strong French influence, and evoke parallels with music by 18th-century masters, such as D'Anglebert, Rameau and Couperin. The two-voice section in mm. 3–5, with its plaintive suspensions, leads to an emotionally charged ascending phrase that culminates in m. 7, following which the dramatic tension is resolved in a serene, yet meaningful conclusion. A *cantabile, legato* touch and subtle phrasing in keeping with the stress-resolution effect in suspensions and appoggiaturas are required to express the reflective mood of this haunting prelude. Light touches of sustain and soft pedal will help with phrasing, tone color, and sound prolongation in the rather slower tempo that befits the pensive character of the music. The use of pedal in the music of Bach ultimately should be left to the performer's taste and individual musical interpretation.

Prelude in C Major, BWV 933

The eighth-note rests should not prevent the theme from unfolding throughout the two first measures as one single phrase with a clear direction toward the melodic leap of the sixth in the second beat of m. 2. The bass notes in the pairs of two eighth notes will benefit from *tenuto* accents as well as potentially holding them a little longer. Forming a horizontal line in the lower layer not only will provide a solid harmonic foundation for the cascading sequences, but will also bring a sense of direction and lead to the application of suitable dynamic fluctuations.

Prelude in C minor, BWV 934

The key signature and rhythmic structure of this prelude point to the style of a minuet. A moderately flowing pace with a light stress on the downbeats will convey the dance character of the piece. Upon analyzing this piece harmonically, we realize that in the majority of measures, the second and/or third beats act as passing tones over the same chord. Though in this way, the phrasing should de-emphasize the second and third beats. Using stress-resolution phrasing in the beginnings of mm. 2 and 4 will further strengthen the rhythmic feel, placing the necessary emphasis and rebound energy on the downbeats.

Prelude in D minor, BWV 935

Perhaps a precursor to the invention, BWV 775 in D minor, this prelude bears some common stylistic features: short imitative sections alternating with sections where the melody is simply accompanied by eighth notes, the two exchanged between the hands in constant dialogue. The shift of register in the B section and the mirror-like manipulation of the motive in the relative major key offer an opportunity for dynamic contrast. The thematic boldness and the bouncy rhythmic feel call for a rather bright, consistent, yet flexible sound, and the use of non-legato and staccato touch in the eighth notes, in the manner of détaché string bowing technique.

Prelude in D Major, BWV 936

The absence of ornamentation and the time signature 2/4, suggest a rather quick, flowing tempo. Unlike most preludes, the bass here, with the exception of mm. 33–36, does not interact thematically with the theme; it rather follows its own course, meandering through a fine path of chord and passing tones. Bringing out the dynamic contours of the left hand line without overpowering the cheery interplay between the soprano and alto voices will add to the transparency of this lighthearted composition.

Prelude in E Major, BWV 937

Suggestive of an allemande, this prelude is divided into two sections. Rather thematically uniform, the musical interest is generated by the harmonic changes through which the theme is led. The harmonically dense measures lend themselves as excellent opportunities for dynamic and timbre variations; those include m. 5 and mm. 13–16, where secondary dominants give way to denser chords such as iii and ii.

Experiment with various dynamic changes to give proper direction and emphasis in these harmonic events, as well as to convey the changes in mood associated with the secondary-chord areas.

Prelude in E minor, BWV 938

An energetic tempo and a vigorous mood are implied in the constantly rising broken-chord structures culminating with the decisive, bold ascending leap of the octave. The dramatic counter-motion of the left-hand lines should be outlined and given direction and focus. The inquisitive rhythmic interplay between the right and left hand in mm. 25–28 can be illuminated effectively by stressing the syncopated eighth notes in the right hand against the flowing ascending line of the bass.

Prelude in C Major, BWV 939

The presence of the tonic and dominant pedal points, and the spinning out of the simple motive in broken-chord tones in ascending motion give this charming prelude an extemporaneous quality. A rather obvious structural harmonic point is the graceful movement to the dominant area through the ii7/V-V7/V-V chord progression in mm. 7–9. A slight *diminuendo* in this transition will spare enough dynamic room for the ensuing ascending melodic line. The final flourish in m. 14 will come across more convincingly by applying a discreet rubato followed by a lengthening of the tempo in the last two measures.

Prelude in C minor, BWV 999

Intended as a lute piece, this prelude is perfectly transferable to the piano. The syncopated feel of the right-hand sixteenth notes in the third beat of each measure, suggestive of lute technique, will be more convincingly articulated in a light *staccato*. Pedal points at the basis of the unfolding harmonic progression and various suspensions result in dramatic dissonances that add pathos and excitement to this seemingly unpretentious prelude. More than just applying dynamics, it is essential to internalize these moments of heightened harmonic tension, in a way that directing the sound toward and away from them will occur more naturally and integrally.

Prelude in D minor, BWV 940

In the style of the French Overture, this somber and majestic prelude displays a constant interaction and motivic exchange between the voices. Since the two upper voices are within close proximity, the performer should distinguish them with more dynamic contrast. The sixteenth note following the dotted eighth, in accordance with the characterization of the French Overture, needs to be boldly enunciated and given enough rhythmic energy. The rhythmic convention of over dotting the eighths is an interpretative option here and, as such, is left to the performer's taste and desired musical intention.

Prelude in E minor, BWV 941

The suspensions and ensuing resolutions in this piece are vital elements contributing to the expressiveness of this prelude. The beginnings of the motive in mm. 11–15 should be articulated distinctly with a light emphasis, the first of the arpeggiated notes being the ending of the previous phrase. Played in tempo, the last note of the triplet in m. 21 would end up sounding almost together with the second of the two eighth notes in the lower voices.

Prelude in A minor, BWV 942

The leaping dance gestures of this gigue-like prelude will be aided by applying *staccato* in the first eighth note of each three-note group; this will also showcase the increasing descending intervals from the fourth to the seventh. In mm. 12–14, the rich chromaticism and mirror-like contrary motion between the motive and the counter theme heighten the drama in a way that the culminating flourish of mm. 15 and 16 comes as a relief of tension.

Prelude in C Major, BWV 943

The mirror-like inversion of the motive, such as seen in mm. 17 and 35, allows Bach to create clear contrapuntal lines and to explore the entire range of the keyboard, leading the motive all the way down to the lower register and often keeping the outer voices quite far apart. In line with C.P.E. Bach's advice to disconnect large intervals, playing the leap of the octave *non-legato* or *staccato* will better define each motivic entrance and will shed light on the wonderful motion of the different lines. The *stretto* entrances of the motive in mm. 48–50 forecast the ensuing fugues in the *Little Fugues* and *Little Preludes with Fugues* that follow this series of preludes.

A special note of thanks to my friends Carol Klose for her invaluable advice and help with the performance notes, and Chris Pawlicki, technical assistant of the music library at the University of Illinois, Urbana-Champaign, for his help in locating the original sources for the music.

References

Bach, Johann Sebastian. *Clavier-Büchlein vor Wilhelm Friedemann Bach*. Edited in facsimile with a preface by Ralph Kirkpatrick. New Haven: Yale University Press, 1959.

Bach, Carl Philipp Emanuel. *Essay on the True Art of Playing Keyboard Instruments*. Edited and translated by William J. Mitchel. New York: W.W. Norton & Company, Inc., 1949.

Couperin, François. *L'Art de Toucher le Clavecin*. Edited and translated by Margery Halford. Van Nuys, CA: Alfred Publishing Co., Inc., 1974.

Ferguson, Howard. *Keyboard Interpretation from the 14th to the 19th Century*. New York and London: Oxford University Press, 1975.

Geiringer, Karl. Johann Sebastian Bach. *The Culmination of an Era*. New York: Oxford University Press, 1966.

Sources for the music contained in this edition:

Neun Kleine Präludien, BWV 924–932. Bach Johann Sebastian. *Neue Ausgabe Sämtlicher Werke (Neue Bach Ausgabe)*, Series V, vol. 5. Bärenreiter Kassel, Basel, London, New York. 1962.

Sechs Kleine Präludien für Anfänger auf dem Klavier, BWV 933–938. Bach Johann Sebastian. *Neue Bach Ausgabe*, Series V, vol. 9. Bärenreiter Kassel, Basel, London, New York, 1999.

Fünf Kleine Präludien, BWV 939–943 and Präludium BWV 999. *Bach Gesellschaft Ausgabe*, vol. 36. Breitkopf & Härtel 1890, republished by Gregg International Publishers, Hans, England, 1968.

Audio Credits

Recorded December 2010 – January 2011 at the home of the editor on his Bechstein concert grand EN 177650. Produced by Christos Tsitsaros. Engineered, edited, mixed, and mastered by Christopher Ericson. Piano Technician: Steve Rasch.

NINETEEN LITTLE PRELUDES

Prelude in C Major

Johann Sebastian Bach
BWV 924

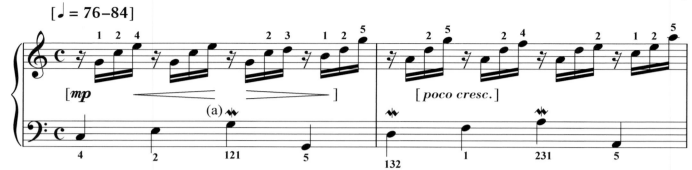

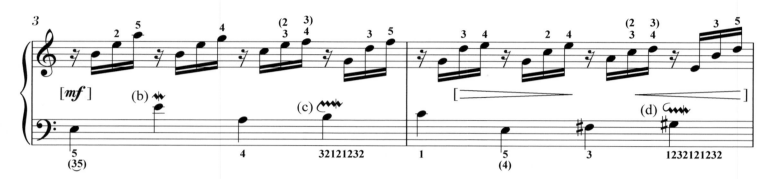

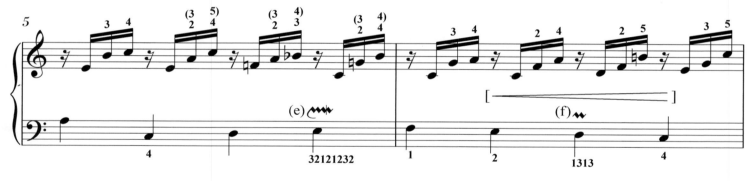

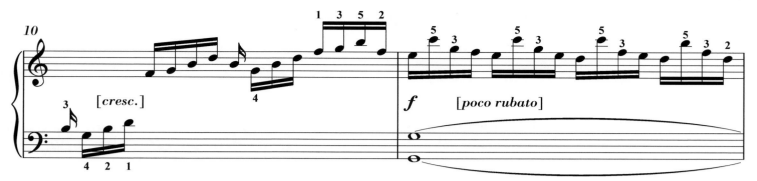

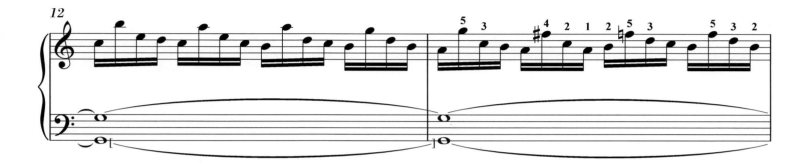

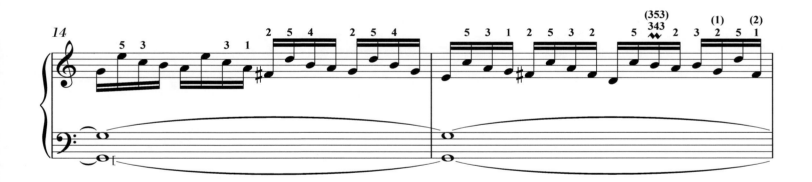

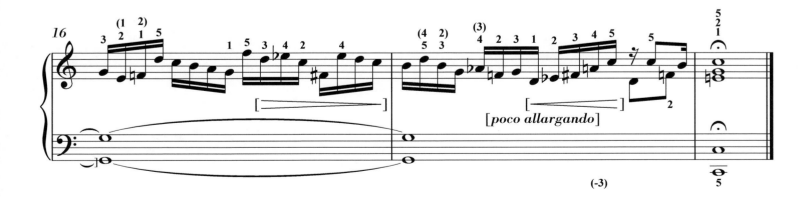

Prelude in D minor

Johann Sebastian Bach
BWV 926

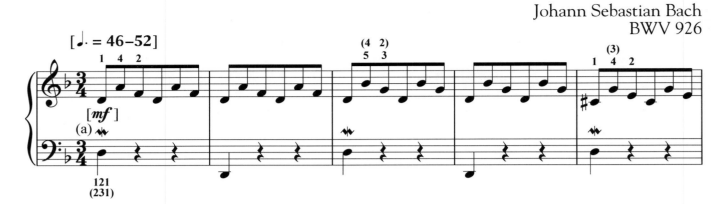

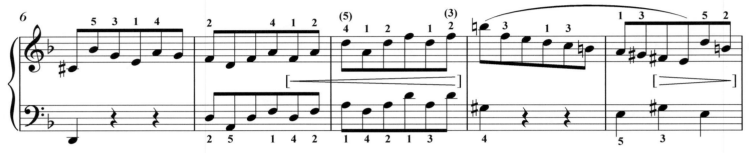

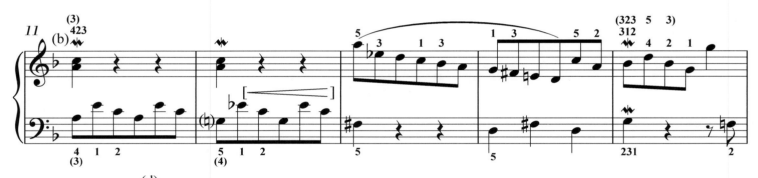

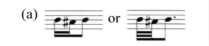

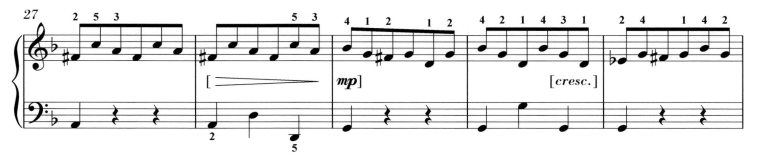

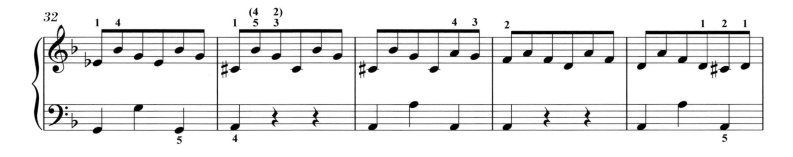

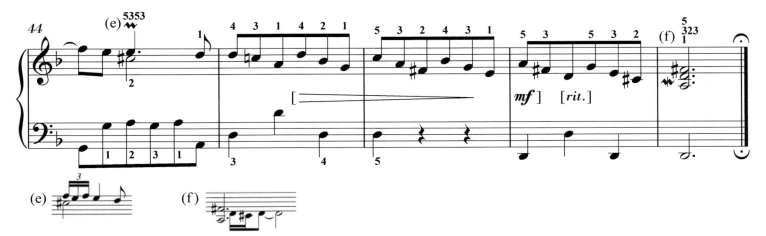

Prelude in F Major

Johann Sebastian Bach
BWV 927

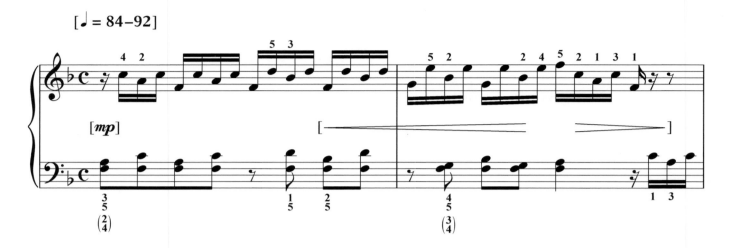

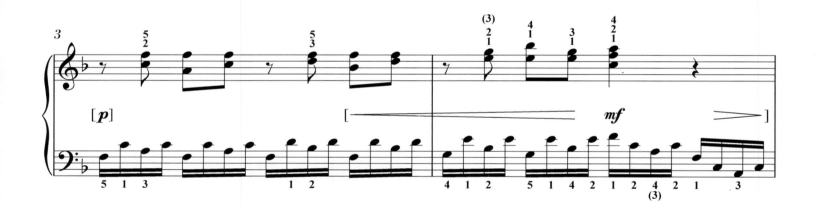

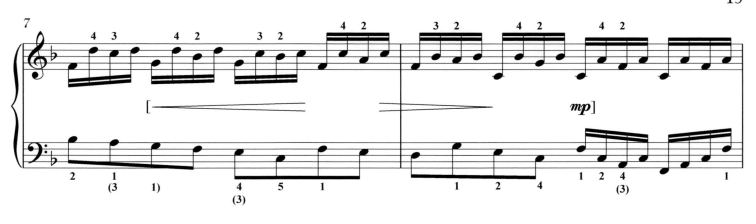

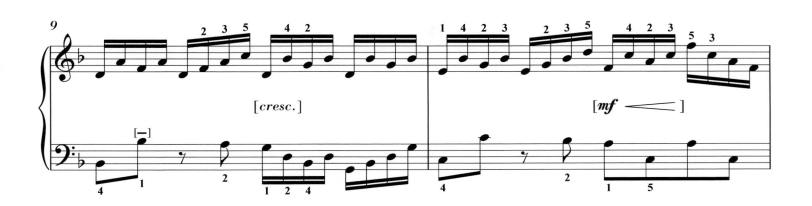

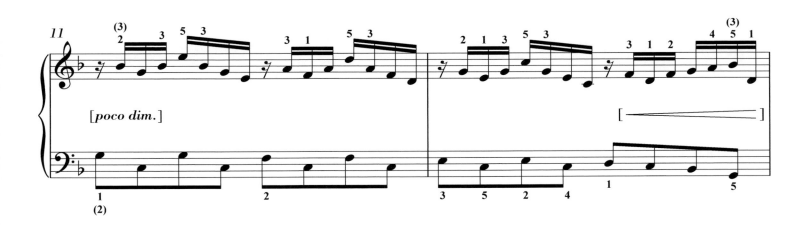

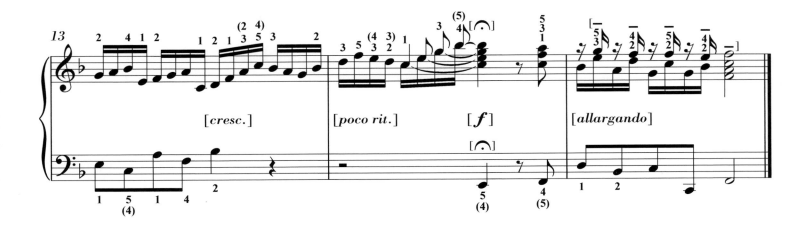

Prelude in G minor

Johann Sebastian Bach
BWV 930

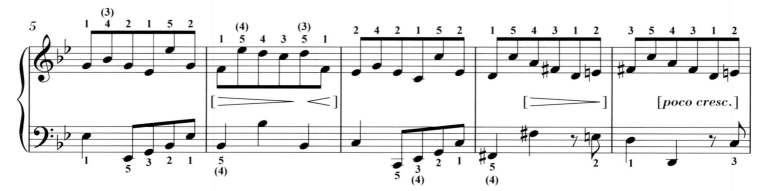

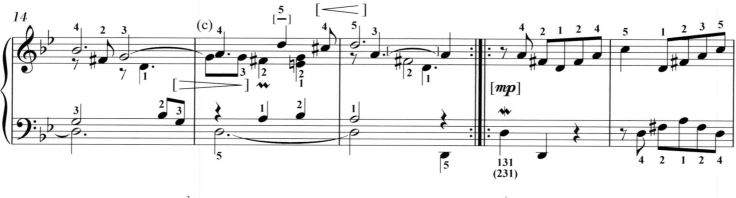

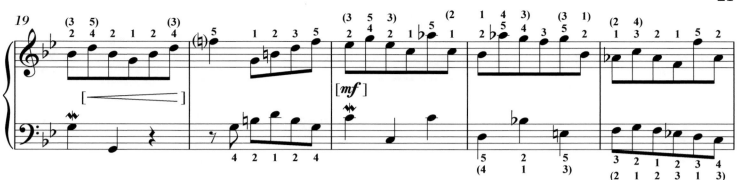

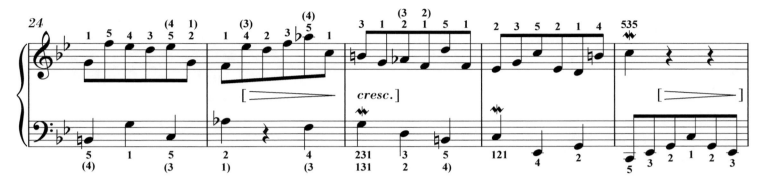

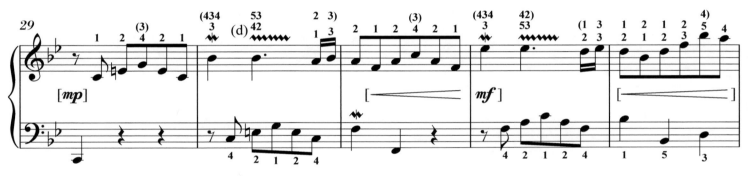

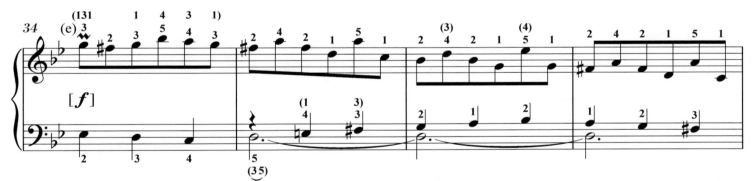

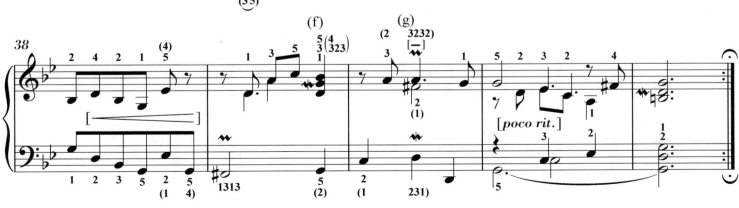

Prelude in F Major

Johann Sebastian Bach
BWV 928

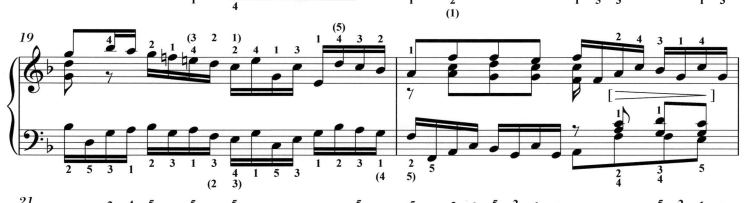

Prelude in D Major

Assumedly by Wilhelm Friedemann Bach
BWV 925

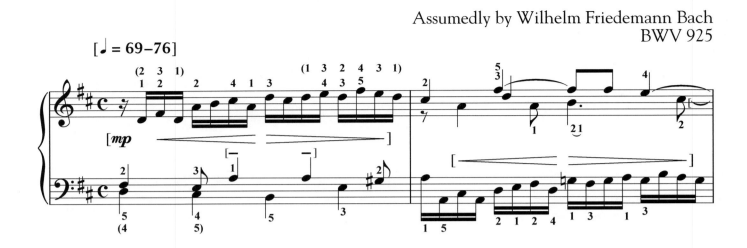

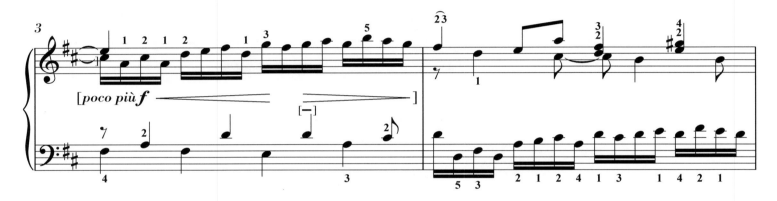

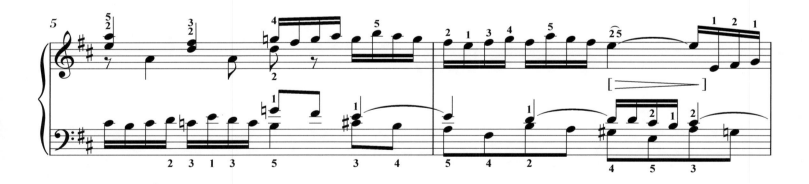

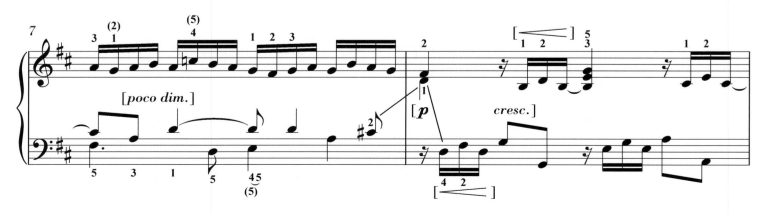

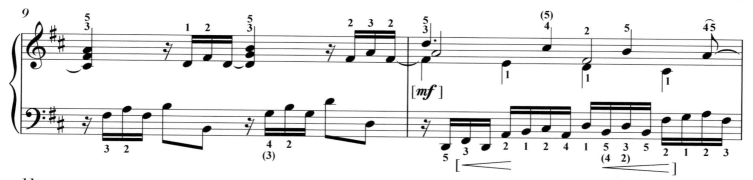

Prelude in A minor

Composer Unknown
BWV 931

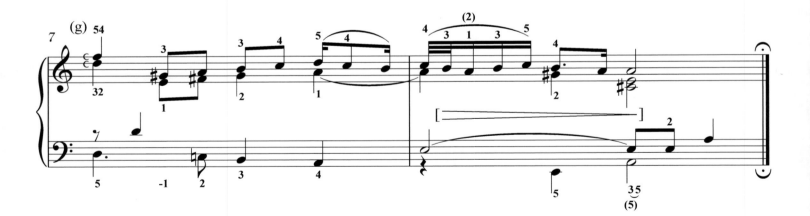

Prelude in C Major

Johann Sebastian Bach
BWV 933

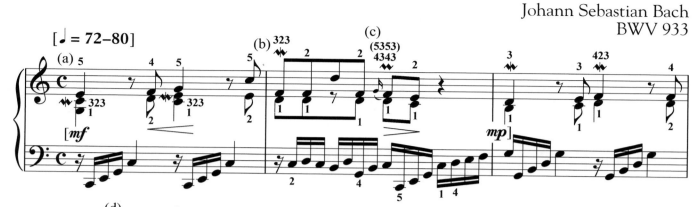

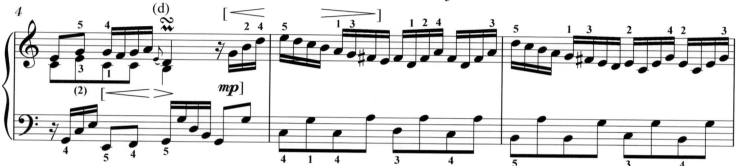

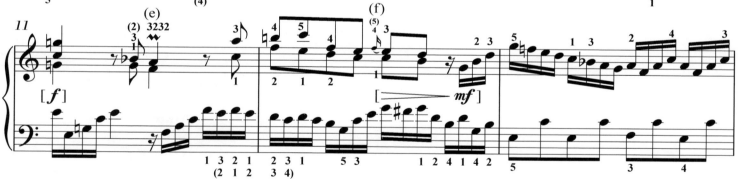

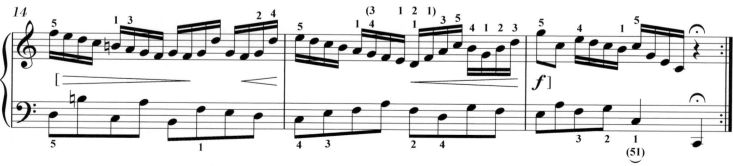

Prelude in C minor

Johann Sebastian Bach
BWV 934

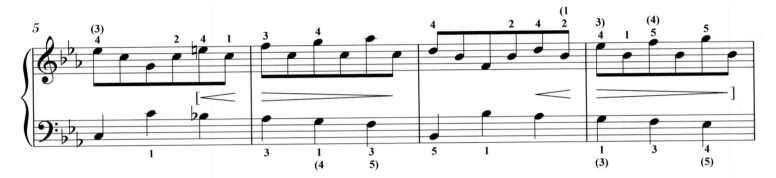

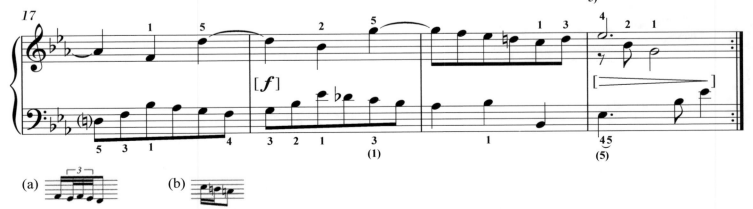

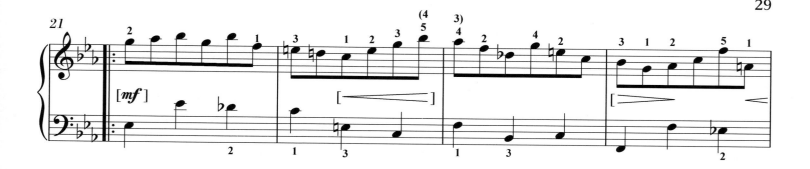

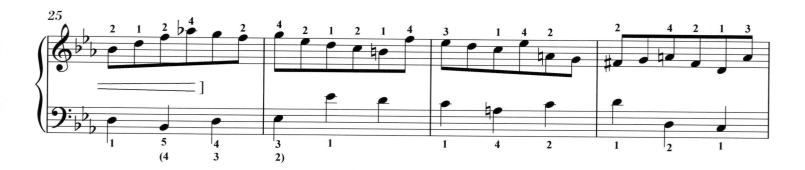

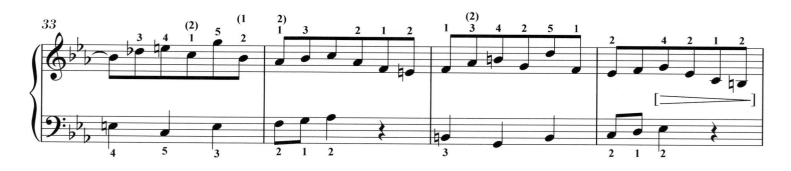

Prelude in D minor

Johann Sebastian Bach
BWV 935

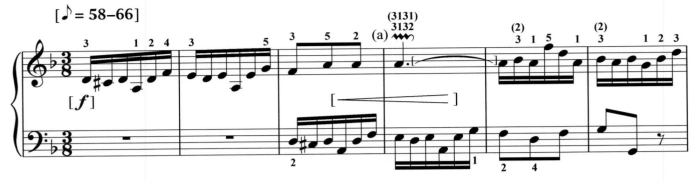

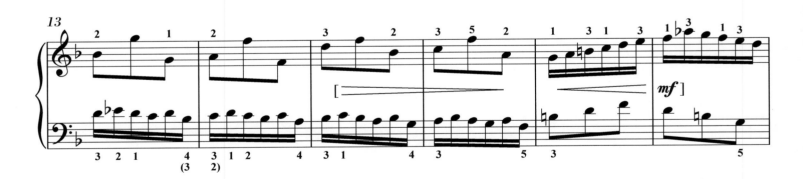

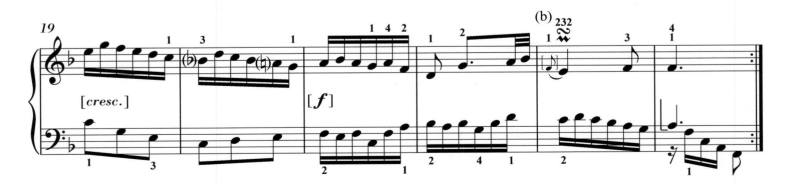

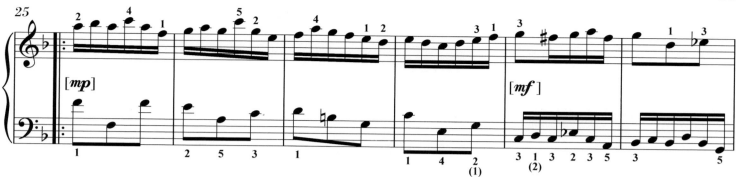

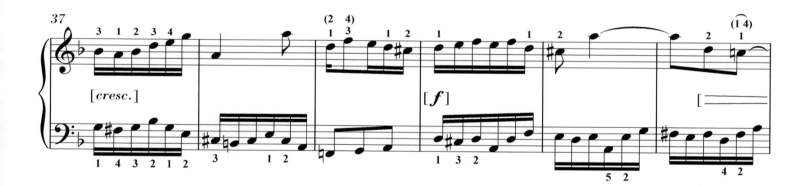

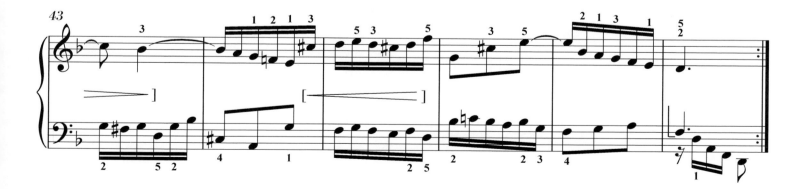

Prelude in D Major

Johann Sebastian Bach
BWV 936

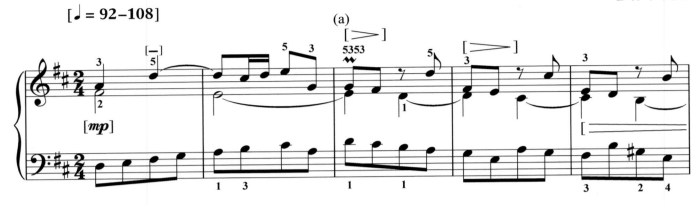

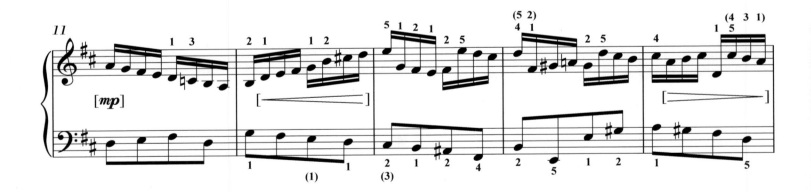

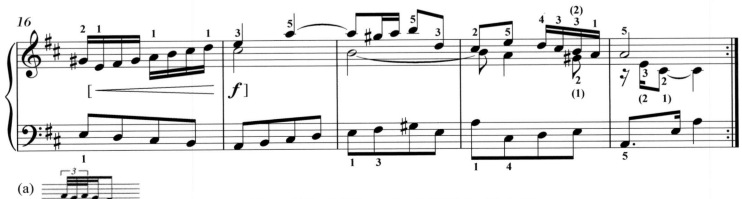

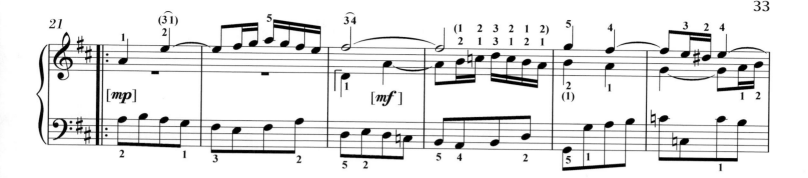

34

Prelude in E Major

Johann Sebastian Bach
BWV 937

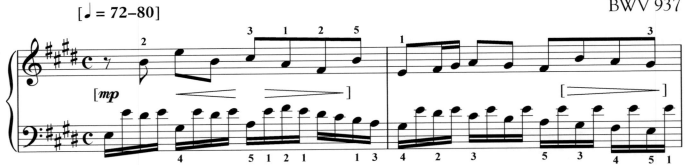

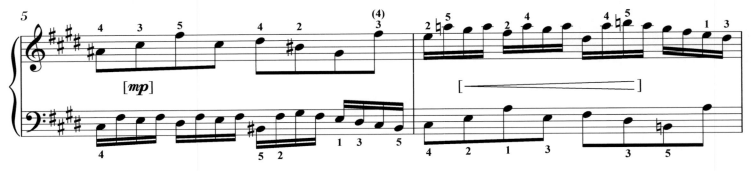

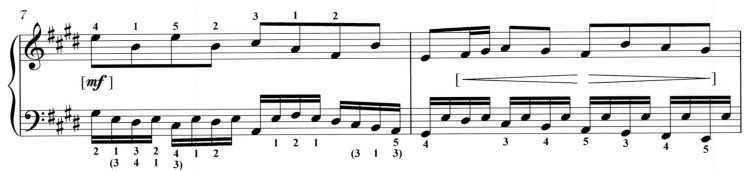

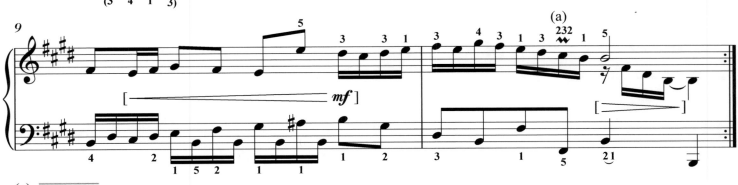

(a)

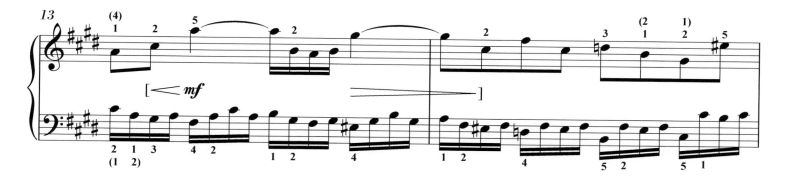

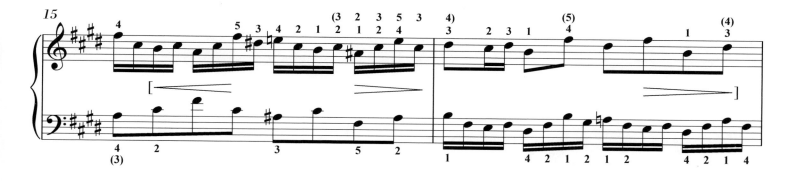

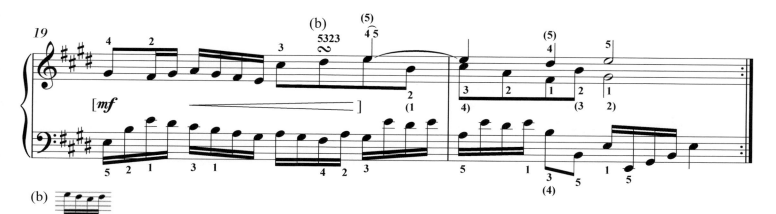

Prelude in E minor

Johann Sebastian Bach
BWV 938

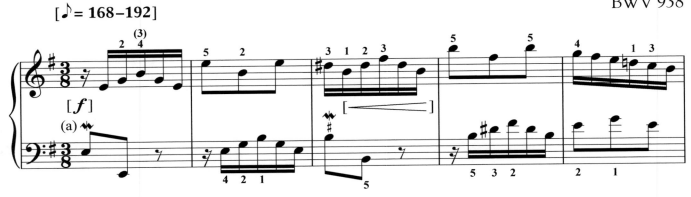

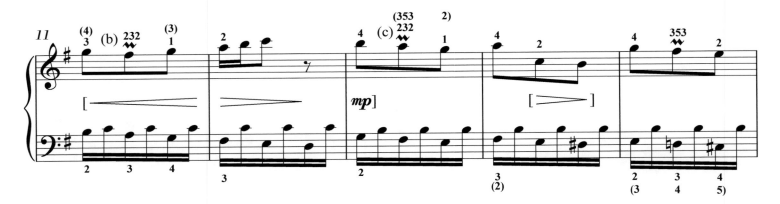

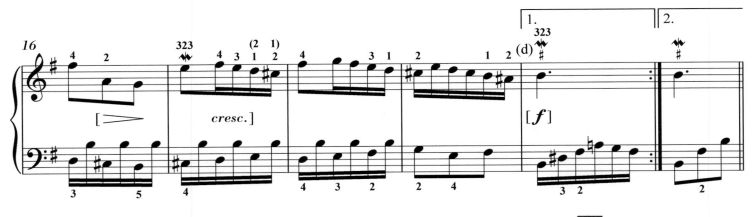

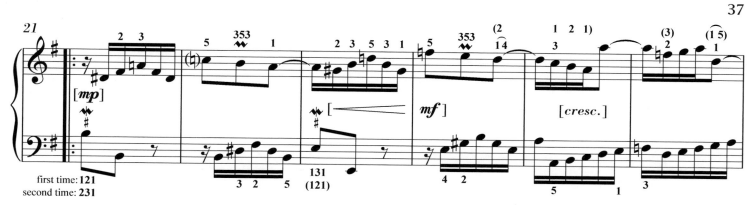

first time: **121**
second time: **231**

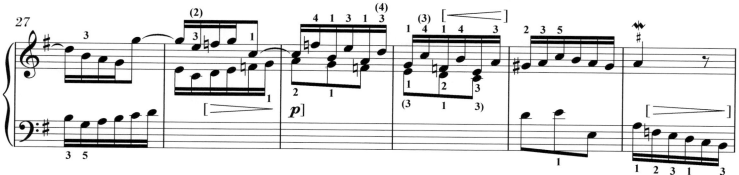

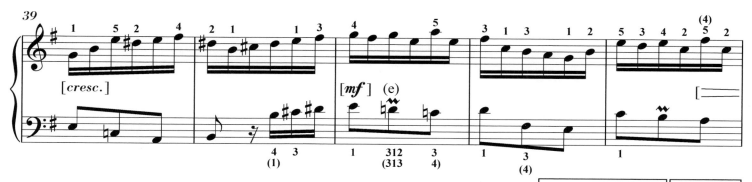

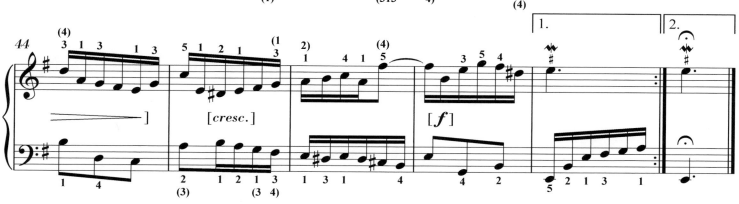

(e) or

Prelude in C Major

Johann Sebastian Bach
BWV 939

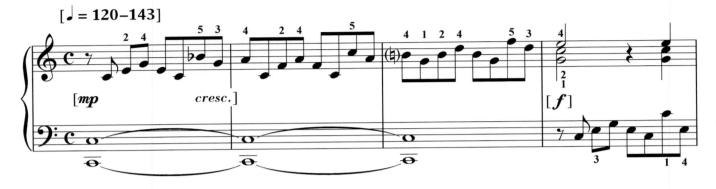

(a)

Prelude in C minor

Johann Sebastian Bach
BWV 999

Prelude in D minor

Johann Sebastian Bach
BWV 940

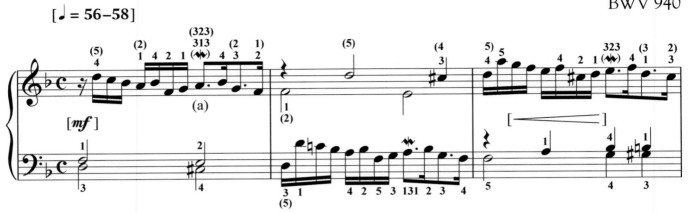

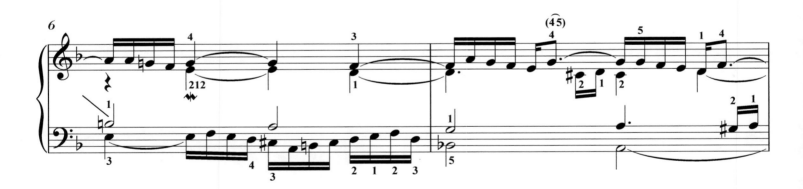

(a)

Prelude in E minor

Johann Sebastian Bach
BWV 941

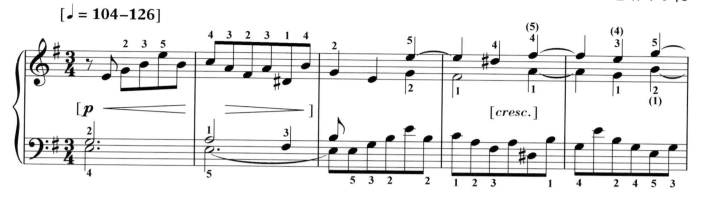

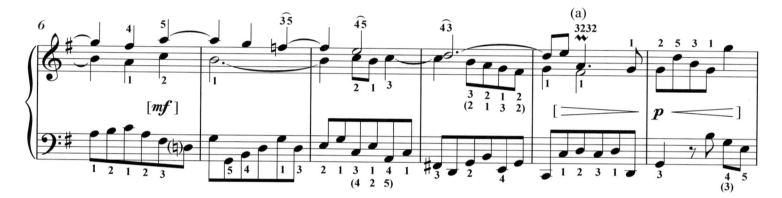

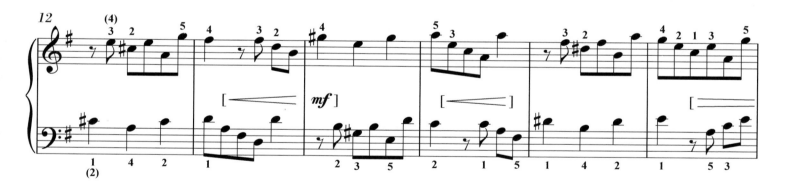

Prelude in A minor

Johann Sebastian Bach
BWV 942

Prelude in C Major

Johann Sebastian Bach
BWV 943

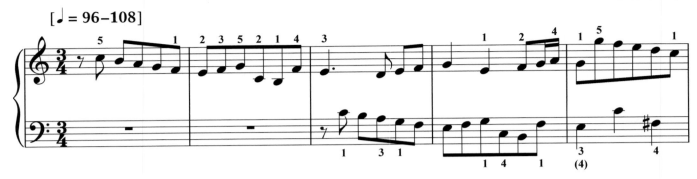

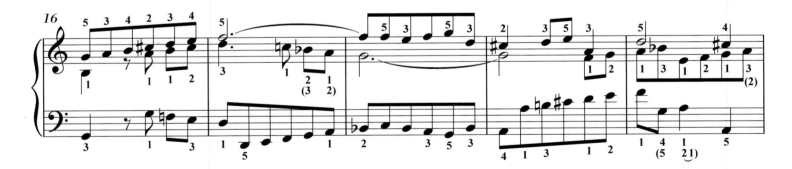

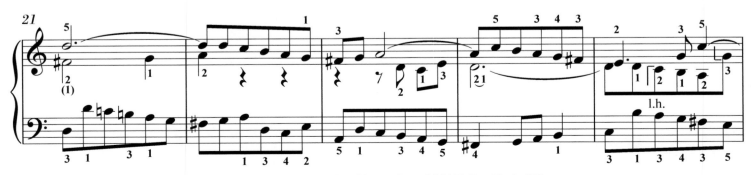

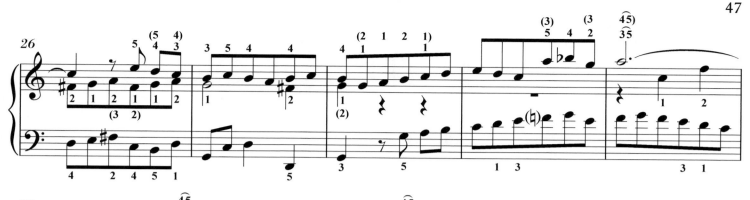

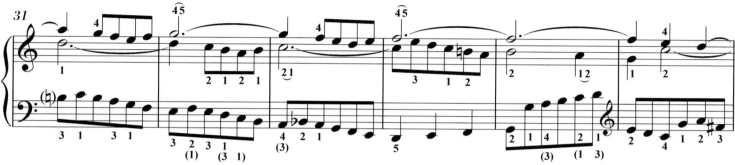

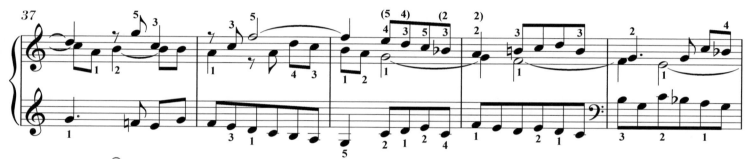

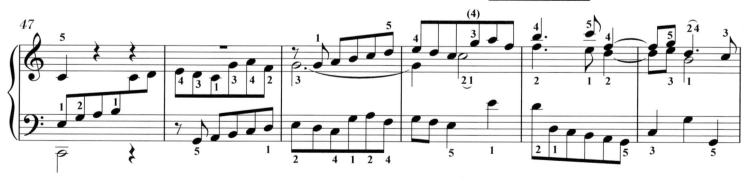

ABOUT THE EDITOR

CHRISTOS TSITSAROS

Christos Tsitsaros, contributing composer and arranger for the Hal Leonard Student Piano Library, was born in Cyprus and received his first formal instruction with Nora Karasik at the Greek Academy of Music of Nicosia, Cyprus. At the age of 13 he won first prize in the National Competition of the Conservatory of Athens. Upon graduating from high school, he moved to Poland where he studied at the Frédéric Chopin Academy in Warsaw. As a result of winning the Gina Bachauer Institution Competition in Athens (1981), he continued his musical studies in Paris and graduated from the Ecole Normale de Musique de Paris, obtaining the Diplôme Supérieur d'Exécution with distinction. A scholarship from the A. G. Leventis Foundation enabled him to pursue further development at the Jacobs School of Music at Indiana University in Bloomington, Indiana, where he received an Artist Diploma and a Master in Music degree (1989). Subsequently, he entered the School of Music at the University of Illinois where he attained a Doctor of Musical Arts in Piano Performance (1993). His mentors include pianists Jan Ekier, Aldo Ciccolini, Germaine Mounier, Jean-Claude Pennetier, Leonard Hokanson, György Sebök, and Ian Hobson.

Dr. Tsitsaros is also quite active as a composer, having won the composition competition at the 1992 National Conference on Piano Pedagogy, which launched an ongoing relationship with Hal Leonard Corporation.

Several of his compositions have been selected by numerous examination systems, including the National Federation of Music Clubs, the RCM examinations of the Royal Conservatory of Music (Toronto), and the Gina Bachauer International Junior Piano Competition.

In 2001, he was artist-in-residence at the Helene Wurlitzer Foundation in New Mexico; the same year, he gave his New York debut recital at Weill Carnegie Hall. He regularly appears in workshops and conferences as a performer and lecturer, and performs as soloist, recitalist, and chamber musician in Europe, the United States, Russia, and Canada. He has participated as a clinician and lecturer for the National Conference on Keyboard Pedagogy, the World Piano Pedagogy Conference, the Music Teachers National Association Conference, and the International Conference on European Music Education (St. Petersburg, Russia).

Christos Tsitsaros is currently Professor of Piano Pedagogy at the University of Illinois in Urbana-Champaign. He also serves as Piano Chair for the Illinois State Music Teachers Association.

Four individual solo albums of his original piano works appear under the Centaur Records label (1998, 2007, 2011).